• • •

The Behavioral Economics Approach to Winning New Clients (and Keeping the Ones You Have!)

The Behavioral Economics Approach to Winning New Clients (and Keeping the Ones You Have!)

Warren Cormier

ISBN-13: 9781983605093
ISBN-10: 1983605093
Library of Congress Control Number: 2018900792
CreateSpace Independent Publishing Platform
North Charleston, South Carolina

Contents

Introduction:

● ● ●

Leveraging the Three Most Powerful Behavioral Dynamics to Your Advantage

In the first *Indiana Jones* film, Indy is confronted in a dusty and crowded Cairo marketplace by a menacing foe brandishing a large, curved scimitar. Indy stands there empty-handed. Things look bad for our hero. Oddly, he looks unafraid, completely confident in the outcome. Suddenly, Indy—looking almost irritated—pulls out a large gun, dispatches his foe with one shot, and calmly walks away.

The barriers to gaining new client relationships are the scimitar-wielding foes.

Around the world, even the most sophisticated companies are entering the battle as the person swinging the sword. They frequently enter the sales-and-marketing fray with commoditized products and undifferentiated brands. I am referring to their physical widgets and services as well as their people. Advisers, agents, sales representatives, and service reps often fight to differentiate an otherwise unspectacular product or service. At some level, we are all trying to market something—or ourselves—to others. Workers sell their labor to employers, advisers sell their expertise to clients, agents sell their know-how and networks, and so on.

On the battlefield, in the free market of ideas, companies spend billions on identifying and reaching needs-driven markets, developing solutions to problems that may or may not be perceived or even real, and engineering new product and service designs. But the velocity of innovation is so rapid that soon after its introduction, a great idea or product is sufficiently copied—and then commoditized so as to eliminate the innovator's competitive advantage. Yes, there are patents and copyrights. But it seems there is often a way to navigate around them or to create a product that is sufficiently similar without violating the copyright and then claim superiority.

Product-feature differentiation as a growth strategy almost always fails in the long run. Many times it fails sooner. Selling product features typically serves to commoditize the product category. Everyone has a new whistle or bell to tack on to the side of the original idea or product design. If your ideas and products are effective in taking market share, competitors will have found a reasonably comparable whistle or bell within months. In a beauty contest, there is always someone just as attractive—or even more attractive. Yet marketers often sell in an uncreative way, relying ultimately on price differences and concessions to close the deal.

"Well," you may ask, "isn't the brand the next point of attack in the battle for differentiation?" Yes, definitely. However, recognition is often just a simplistic way of distinguishing brands. Most brands are not differentiated by what attributes they represent and what promises they make to the market. Unfortunately, many sellers believe their brand is differentiated when it's not. In these cases, their biggest foes are themselves. So if your products and brands are not differentiated, are you dead in the water? No!

Behavioral economics has a solution. Knowing what you are really selling—and understanding what problems you are really solving—provides a formidable edge in the battle to capture new clients and keep those you already have. Anyone bringing a gun to a knife fight has a much higher chance of prevailing. Importantly, these solutions apply to you as a person seeking to establish and retain any type of professional relationship.

Before we get into the specific lessons, it is important to recognize the three most powerful behavioral elements when trying to change how people act. Conventional wisdom says the most powerful behavioral factors are fear and greed. Our research reveals that neither of those top the list. Instead, our research shows that the three most powerful factors are:

* Trust
* Aversion to Loss
* Avoiding Regret

Let's start with trust. Our models show that building trust is the most powerful way to change behavior. Trustworthiness is also the most important selection factor among a group of equally qualified competitors. What exactly do we mean by "trust"?

Trust is primal. It is an integral component of human evolution. Without it a civilization cannot flourish. Today more than ever, as we sift through an avalanche of information available on the Internet, knowing whom and what to trust (and not to trust) is essential. We look for signals of trustworthiness in every interaction. Even now, as you read, you are looking for signs that you can trust what is written. Trust allows people to engage and take risks. Most importantly, trust allows people to act in ways that may not seem familiar, intuitive, or safe. Trust is the foundation upon which loyalty is built and sustained.

Later in this book you will read that you and/or your product are unknown entities to the prospect. Hiring you or adopting your product is an act of risk-taking behavior. Your job in the sales process is creating trust and reducing the sense of your riskiness. Unfortunately, if you are in the financial-services industry, trust is lowest compared to other industries such as health care, IT, and consumer packaged goods. Not working to build trust in a new relationship can be fatal. We often hear prospects express trust as "chemistry." Without it, your chances of being selected are slim. Keep in mind that in the highly technical field of financial advice, for example, prospects do not know what they feel they should know to make a decision. The same is true if you are picking a brain surgeon. Trust becomes paramount in these circumstances.

Aversion to loss is another critically important dynamic to understand. It is so important that it won a Nobel Prize for Dr. Daniel Kahneman, Eugene Higgins professor of psychology, emeritus, and professor of psychology and public affairs, emeritus, at Princeton University. Aversion to loss is the foundational idea of "prospect theory" and can be simply explained as a loss having substantially more negative psychological impact than a gain of an equal amount. In fact, a loss has over twice the impact as a gain of an equal amount.

Knowing this is important in understanding that your prospect's decision may well be based on taking the safe route that minimizes the possibility of a negative outcome, even though you may feel you presented an overwhelming case for your superiority.

Third, people want to avoid the feeling of regret for an action they have taken. Importantly, they integrate this need into their actual decisions. Nobody wants to feel they made a bad decision, even if all the evidence supported it. Your goal is twofold: reducing the sense of possible regret for picking you and increasing the sense of possible regret for not picking you. It bears repeating that in the highly technical field of financial advice, prospects do not know what they feel they should know to make a decision.

One last point on regret versus fear. They may seem similar, but they are very different. Fear overweights small chances of something happening, while regret simply states the highly likely result of an action taken. Consider the example of childhood vaccinations causing autism. Simply by stating the possible link between the two, the possibility is grossly overstated. Fear is created, and people start taking inadvisable steps. Even worse, fear is amplified when using arguments such as, "There is no scientific evidence that vaccination does not cause autism." Regret simply states the highly likely consequences of an action. For example, if you don't save enough for retirement, you may have a less pleasant retirement lifestyle.

Trust. Aversion to loss. Avoiding regret. We will return to these important concepts in the chapters ahead. Keep them in mind as you contemplate how to use behavioral economics to your advantage.

Finally, I want to extend a special thanks to pioneers in behavioral economics such as Drs. Daniel Kahneman, Richard Thaler, Shlomo Benartzi, and Dan Ariely, whose work has enlightened us all as to how the world works. I also want to thank Tim Kohn, Ashish Shrestha, and Adam Martin of Dimensional Fund Advisors for their encouragement and assistance, without which this book never would have become a reality.

Part One:
Rewriting the Ground Rules

Lesson 1

● ● ●

Start Your Pitch with a Surprise Ending

If you're in a fair fight, you didn't plan it properly.

—*Nick Lappos, chief R&D pilot, Sikorsky Aircraft*

Fight? What fight? What if there isn't a fight? Do you need to create the fight? Many times—in fact, most times—prospects do not even realize they're prospects. They are perfectly happy with their world as it relates to your ideas or products. They are in an equilibrium that feels comfortable. That equilibrium usually involves a high level of loyalty to existing, trusted providers—and those are the people you are trying to replace. In fact, the only one who isn't happy may be you. So your goal is to convince prospects they're really not as happy as they think—that their bliss may be based on ignorance. Physics tells us that upsetting an equilibrium usually takes a huge amount of energy, like a two-by-four between the eyes.

Starting the fight means convincing the prospect there is a new, better equilibrium. OK, so how?

"Thought leadership" is one key to getting the fight started. I know, it is an overused phrase. But few people really know what it means, how to prove it, what it looks like, why it makes relationships sticky (see **Lesson 2** on adding value and **Lesson 6** on building loyalty). Prospects sometimes say they are prospects because they fear that they aren't even aware of an entirely different solution to problems they face. They often say they are not even sure if there are problems they are not aware of. Fear of the unknown can be a powerful equilibrium-breaking force and may be at work every day in their lives.

When you can fully identify those unknowns, you become invaluable to those prospects. If you can position yourself as that guiding light about the highly likely threats they face—and not just a technical adviser—you become a partner in their success. At that point, recognizing your thought leadership, people become very comfortable that you are aware of their situation and their existing weaknesses or any new ones that are lurking. Importantly, we are not suggesting creating fear, but instead helping to assuage prospects' fears.

Behavioral economics also tells us that people fear failure and loss more than they revel in success of an equal magnitude. A simple experiment conducted by Drs. Shlomo Benartzi, Sheena Iyengar, and Alex Previtero illustrates the point. Three separate groups of people were asked if they would prefer a guaranteed $500 or a 15 percent chance of winning $10,000 (group 1), a 15 percent chance of winning $100,000 (group 2), or a 15 percent chance of winning $1 million (group 3). Keep in mind that the expected value of the first alternative is $1,500, and the second and third alternatives are $15,000 and $150,000, respectively.

1 Making tradeoffs more tangible

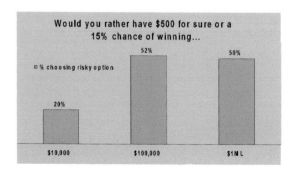

Would you rather have $500 for sure or a
15% chance of winning...

□ % choosing risky option

52%	50%	
20%		
$10,000	$100,000	$1M L

Source: Benartzi, Iyengar and Previtero (in progress)   31

Amazingly, only 20 percent would take the chance at $10,000, and half would take the chance at $100,000. Furthermore, raising the stakes to $1 million had no impact on risk-taking.

The point is that people are more afraid of regretting making a bad choice. Therefore, you have to position yourself as the safe and the right bet.

To get this fight started, you have to say something new that will get the prospect thinking about just how the world could look or about if there is a new dimension they can't see. You must have a surprise ending to the tired sales pitches that prospects hear every day. In his book, *Made to Stick: Why Some Ideas Survive and Others Die*, Dr. Chip Heath of Stanford University points out that ideas that catch on are those that defy conventional thinking, make people think differently, and most importantly, alter their behavior. In fact, this is a great definition of thought leadership: an idea that makes people think differently about a familiar subject or problem—*and* compels people to take an action.

What are some of those persuasive ideas pointed out by Dr. Heath? You only use 10 percent of your brain, a ludicrous idea. Your hotel key card has your credit card information and your Facebook password, causing people to keep their cards after they check out. A famous story that stuck is the one about the business traveler who accepts a drink from an attractive stranger in a bar. The next thing he remembers, he is in a bathtub of ice and he sees a note saying "call 911." He calls 911, and the operator is unfazed and asks if there is a tube coming from his back. The man says, "Yes!" and the operator says, "Sir, your kidney was harvested by a gang of organ thieves." People who hear this story change their behavior the next time an attractive stranger offers them a drink.

See Chip Heath on YouTube

http://www.youtube.com/watch?v=Bs9NbxJHV-w

Summary: *Chip examines why certain ideas—ranging from urban legends to folk medical cures—survive and prosper in the social marketplace of ideas. Why is it that urban legends stick in the backs of our minds? And why is it that you can't get that clever little auto insurance commercial out of your head? Chip will answer these questions and help you, as a leader or marketer, create messages that will break through the larger marketplace of ideas and stick to what's important.*

Let's be honest: the last brochure you read, the last telemarketer call you received, the last "Lunch-and-Learn" you attended, or the last news story on CNN you saw will probably not change the way you think or how you behave and will soon be forgotten. Put another way, you need an idea that will change the way your prospect—who is in equilibrium—thinks and behaves. Without it, you're wasting your and your prospect's time. In simple terms, you have to become relevant.

Lesson 2

● ● ●

From the First Contact, Start Adding Value

*A poor relation is the most **irrelevant** thing in nature.*

—CHARLES LAMB, ENGLISH ESSAYIST, POET, AND ANTIQUARIAN

I can't get the prospect to give me even five minutes.

—MOST SALESPEOPLE

In our research of sales successes and failures over the past thirty years, the fact that prospects don't have time to engage is one of the most cited reasons salespeople give for why they can't meet their quotas. That is, along with, "Our price is too high." (I'll deal with that excuse later.) But guess what? Your prospects really are very busy every day. Someone or something is getting their time. So you need to get yourself on the list of "Top Ten Things the Prospect Needs to Worry about Today." Yes, these lists exist, at least in the minds of your prospects. And, importantly, these lists are being reordered minute by minute.

Let's look at the top ten things that got your attention yesterday. Write them down and include how much time you spent on each item. Then, using a 1–10 scale, rate how relevant those things were to your long-term success (10 is high).

"The Top Ten Things that Got My Attention Yesterday"		
Item	Time Spent on It	Long-Term Relevance

Now, look at the list and ask yourself if "meeting with a salesperson I have no relationship with who has nothing new to tell me and wants to talk about himself" would make your list. Now add to the list what you have to offer that would get you on the list. How about, "Provide insights that would change the way the prospect thinks and influence his or her behavior"?

If prospects say they're too busy to meet you, there is a reason. You failed to make yourself relevant. When we analyze what gets on the top ten list, almost all of the things are directly tied to something about advancing their personal or corporate success. OK, makes sense. So why can't you get in the top ten? It often has to do with the message you are delivering in the come-on. When I perform behavioral analysis of lead paragraphs in marketing materials (approach letters, brochures, websites, and so on), the message is almost always about the seller, not the buyer. This is a mistake. Buyers *don't care about your past successes. They care about their future successes.*

Let's take a look at a typical come-on focused on the seller, not the buyer:

* Our firm was founded in 1863.
* We are headquartered in New York City, with more than eighty-five thousand employees in offices around the world.

*   Our firm services approximately twenty-two million customers worldwide.

Never before in modern economic history has the saying, "Prospects don't care what you have to say until they know you care about them" been truer. Find something they want to think about. What do people want to hear about? Them or you? Prospects always want to hear a story with themselves as the main character. Specifically, how will the prospect's life be better because he or she picked you to have a meeting? If you are not relevant, the client will give you signals, besides yawning and looking at his/her watch. Is the prospect asking meaningful questions? Is the prospect discussing scenarios that include you in the future of the company? Is the prospect argumentative? Essentially, is the prospect listening or reloading? Can't think of anything? Maybe there isn't a way you can improve his or her life. Or maybe you're not thinking hard enough about it.

Here is an example of an approach letter and why it fails to create relevance.

Dear Susan,

    By way of introduction I represent XYZ company, a leader in XXXXX innovation and production. We have been successfully meeting the needs of major players in your industry for 150 years. At your convenience, we would like to come to your offices to share our capabilities and discuss how we can meet the pressing needs you have.

Sounds reasonable, right? Wrong. There is almost no place for the buyer in this letter. It's all about the seller's wants and needs. It is presenting information about you, the seller. Nowhere does it tell the buyers what you know about them or just how their lives will be better as a result of having the meeting. No sale.

Then how do you become relevant? From the first contact, start adding value. If you are as good as you say you are, you know what is keeping your prospect up at night. Offer up a "free meatball." How do you feel when the restaurant waiter brings a free amuse-bouche? Or a free dessert? We all love it! And the chef, who sent it out to you, is suddenly relevant to you. Prospects tell us all the time they love getting something of value for free. You probably do too. Instant relevance. What do you see at every table in a vendor exhibitor hall at a business conference? Brochures? Yes. Product samples? Yes. Tchotchkes? Definitely. And what are visitors looking at most? The tchotchkes: golf balls, flashlights, pens, change purses, rubber earths. They pick up off the table what is of value to them. I watched at a conference recently for several breaks. Everyone leaves the exhibit hall with multiple tchotchkes; few are carrying brochures. What the meatball is depends on the situation, but here is an example of an approach letter offering a great meatball:

> *Dear Susan,*
>
> *XXXXX (the prospect's firm), as others, likely will be severely affected by the new banking legislation. I have compiled new information on how the thought leaders in the insurance and legal industries are dealing with the potential threats you may face and how to mitigate them. I have attached an outline of my findings and would be happy to elaborate on them at any time with you and your staff. Also, please attend a webinar I am hosting on the "Ten Hidden Risks Created by the New Legislation." I will follow up next week by telephone.*

Instant relationship, relevance, value added, demonstration of competence, reduced risk of engaging with you, increased risk of not engaging with you, partnering, chemistry, trust. Essentially, a reason to put you on the list of the top ten people the prospect should talk to today. The prospect has put you on his or her team before you even get the business.

What if you provide the information and the prospect claims he/she already knew it? I've heard that one before, but when information makes sense and is helpful, people often come to the conclusion they already knew it. Fact is, they may have thought they knew it, but now they know they know it.

Lesson 3

● ● ●

Understand to Whom You Are Selling

*Get closer than ever to your customers. So close that you tell
them what they need well before they realize it themselves.*

—STEVE JOBS

To whom are you selling? Do you know or even think about it? What is their role in decision making? The answer is important. Often you have no idea where the person to whom you are selling fits in the decision-making chain. Yet that information may change your pitch. It would be great to know, but it is surprising how often the salesperson doesn't know. The top reason prospects get turned off in a sales process? "The salesperson didn't even understand who I am." So what do I mean by "do you know who your prospect is?" You may have heard the term "psychographics." It simply means what makes people tick. Let's get really specific. I do much of my work in the world of employee benefits. That means I help my clients understand how to sell benefits programs to people in charge of human resources. Here is what I mean by "knowing" your prospect. Here is my clients' psychographic profile:

* Risk averse, fear-driven
* Rules-driven
* Process-reliant
* Project-oriented
* Granular in their thinking (willing to run into the weeds at the expense of losing the big picture)
* Slightly paranoid/suspicious of new providers and concepts that appear too good to be true
* Protective of those they are charged to serve (company and participants)
* Problem solvers
* Empathetic
* Desire to help others
* Weary due to resource constraints (relative to the HR retirement mission)
* Resistant to new programs/processes without a clear quid quo pro that accrues to them
* Prioritizes the needs of the company over the needs of employees
* Loyal to the firm and employees
* Motivated by admiration and recognition of coworkers

Get the idea? If you don't know the psychographic profile of your clients and you have a commoditized product, you are dead in the water. So how do you build the profile? Ask yourself some questions about the prospect. Here is the list of questions:

* Is the prospect looking to go the safe route or find new ways of doing things?
* Is the prospect a totally by-the-book person, or does he or she like to think outside the box?
* Does the prospect hide behind process? ("We have always done it this way.")
* Is the prospect strictly looking at the project at hand or the bigger picture surrounding the project?

* Is the prospect more comfortable focusing on the details and minutiae, or is he or she (also) comfortable looking at the big picture?
* Is the prospect slightly paranoid/suspicious of new providers and concepts or welcoming of new ideas?
* Do you find the prospect to be paternalistic when it comes to those he or she serves?
* Does the prospect seem to be a problem-solver as opposed to living within existing constraints?
* Is the prospect feeling defeated by resource constraints?
* Do all new programs/processes need to have a clear quid quo pro that accrues to the prospect personally?
* Does the prospect place the needs of the company over the needs of employees?
* What motivates the prospect? Advancement, recognition, money, low- stress environments?

If you can answer these questions, you are well on your way to getting the sale. But it is also important to know why. One, the more you know, the more you can tailor your presentation to the prospect's needs, perceived or otherwise. But there is an even more important reason. The more you demonstrate you know about people, the higher the trust they place in you. Trustworthiness is the most important selection factor, by far, especially in the familiar situation of an undifferentiated product. You hear the phrase "a name you can trust" all the time. The prospect has to find a difference that facilitates decision-making. In the absence of something concrete, like a product feature or price, prospects will almost universally revert to how much they trust the salesperson.

Using jargon is a surefire way to diminish trust. You may not even realize you are using jargon or that your prospect doesn't know the jargon. The higher the expertise in a subject, the worse is the "curse of knowledge." We all suffer from this curse. I first ran across this phrase while reading *Made to Stick: Why Some Ideas Survive and Others Die,* coauthored by Dr. Chip Heath, a professor of organizational behavior at Stanford University. Essentially, the curse of knowledge is defined this way: you don't know what it is like not to know what you know.

Jargon does not help to demonstrate your knowledge. In fact, it can show prospects that you know nothing about them. Not speaking in a language the prospect knows lowers trust.

Finally, don't assume your trust level is high. If you are a financial adviser for businesses, for example, our research shows that only 23 percent of B2B customers feel they can trust you to do the right thing most of the time. Not a high bar to leap over, but less than a quarter agree that you do. Trust is earned over time. Always assume you need to build it.

Lesson 4

• • •

Make Them Think Twice about Saying No

You may not think of yourself this way, but to the prospect, you represent a huge risk. *And* you represent a risk the prospect may not be authorized to take. When was the last time you took a risk you didn't need to take or took a risk that didn't have potential reward? You have to persuade the prospect that you aren't risky when you are unknown, untested, and unreliable. By making yourself more known, the perceived risk you represent goes down. Ask yourself, "Am I giving the prospect a sufficient reason to upset his/her world?" I can tell you now that you probably aren't, particularly if you lead your pitch with product features. If prospects are willing to work hard on your behalf, they may figure out what is in it for them. But they won't work hard for you because they don't even know you!

You need to convert your product or idea into a compelling reason for prospects to take the risk when it's not even mandated by their job. Even better, help them understand the risks *of not picking you.* Make them ponder the possible consequences of saying no.

So let's do it. Get back to what makes your prospect tick. You know what your product does and what solutions it represents. More important, how it could make them look better? There was an old Vidal Sassoon ad slogan that said, "If you don't look good, we don't look good." By now, is it becoming obvious that the typical approach of starting a sales interaction by talking about your company and your product features *never* gets you on the "Top Ten Most Relevant People I Need to Talk to Today" list?

Here is the list of proven ways to make you look *risky*:

* Moving too quickly through illustrations
* Claiming to be an expert in many things (broadly stating areas of expertise undermines best-of-breed image)
* Assuming the prospect knows esoteric things
* Speaking in acronyms
* Having no bench strength
* Using an e-mail address that ends in gmail, aol, hotmail, and so on
* Not offering references or client lists
* Stating your firm's time in business (How long in business is long enough? Saying you've been in business 150 years is overkill and begs the question: Why are you not the most successful firm if you've been at it so long?)
* Claiming an enormous number of clients
* Listing too many capabilities and awards, recognitions, and so on desensitizes the prospect—there is always someone with more.

> **KEY TAKEAWAY:** *If you remember one thing from this lesson, it should be that prospects fear a poor customer experience the most, assuming the products live up to their specifications.*

To reduce their sense of this risk, look to the sales process as a proxy to create a clear picture in their mind of life after the contract is signed. That is why the old adage "enthusiasm is key" is so true. Going into the relationship, prospects want to know you really want the business *and* that you fear the loss of the relationship as much as they want it to work. In essence, you might say it's mutually assured destruction.

An effective way to provide that post-contract-signing experience is through syndication. That is, finding a deliverable that represents what you do and how you do it but has low to no cost. Free webinars, multisponsored research, or cosponsored white papers are extremely effective in creating a broader perception of you and your company. Prospects need to take only a small sip of the soup to know if the whole bowl is too hot.

Lesson 5

● ● ●

Know Thyself—and Be Painfully Honest

In **Lesson 3** I wrote about the value of knowing what really makes your prospects tick. Knowing what makes *you* tick is actually just as important. Here are some behavioral concepts for you to consider in figuring that out:

1. What are you comfortable talking about? Product features and prices or feelings?

    This dichotomy is a key barrier to success. I find that most people in a selling situation prefer to talk about empirical aspects of the deal—price charts, feature lists, engineering specifications, and so on. But that information only puts you in the running. It is the intuited, emotional aspects of the process that push you into the win column. There are three stages to a win:

    *   Brand gets you invited to the battle.
    *   Product features and specs get you into the finals.
    *   "Feel" (trust) gets you in the winner's circle.

2. Desperation is a malodorous cologne/perfume.

    What is your greatest fear in this process? Losing money? Loss of self-esteem or admiration? Do you fear loss more than you savor success? How big is the difference? Regardless of your answer, you are communicating it to your prospects. How you deal with rejection not only affects your near-term success but also can destroy or create long-term success. Remember, if you've done an effective job in the sales process, "no" usually means "not now, but I will have you come back next time." Although it may feel good in the moment to tell prospects what you really think of them, it will only destroy future opportunities.

3. Are you drinking the Kool-Aid about yourself? (Remember, you are a product too!)

   What is it about you that increases your chances of *winning* or *losing*? Fill out this table to find out. We will analyze the results in chapter 10, which is focused on commoditization and Kano analysis. Here is an example of a self-assessment:

My Strengths	Effect on Winning	Effect on Losing	Conclusion
Plenty of certifications/ licenses	Zero—because everyone has them	Significant—if you don't have them	Not a differen-tiator

4. Are you listening or reloading?

   Have you fallen in love with your own ideas? If so, you are probably going to end up dead in the water. Are you even tolerant of conflicting views? Do you find yourself hoping that your prospects will stop talking, or even worse, not allowing them to finish a thought? Do you often speak first in a discussion?

> **KEY TAKEAWAY:** *Selling is all about listening for needs, fears, possible toeholds, , and so on. The prospect is typically screaming those needs* at *the top of his or her lungs if you listen. It is usually very subtle.*

Left-Brain-Oriented Example
What the client wants:
"I want peace of mind when I am gone. I want my family to be taken care of. And while I'm still around, I want to have the freedom to pursue my dreams beyond professional or occupational pursuits. I want to come a virtuoso pianist!"

What the adviser says:
"We will listen to your needs and translate them into an investment recommendation. Then we will assess the optimal risk profile of your portfolio."

This is a failure to communicate. The client/prospect will never appreciate how that technical talk translates into his being able to take up piano.

5. Do you really even believe you are the best one for the job?
Sounds like an odd question. But my research on the topic has uncovered the critical importance of this dynamic. Interestingly, prospects can answer the question immediately. Furthermore, they will rarely pick a provider who expresses self-doubt. There are telltale signs that you're giving off, such as failure to make eye contact and unwillingness to discuss recent changes in your organization. Most are too subtle to describe, but they add up to a "feeling" the prospects intuit in their right brains.

6. What are prospects not asking you, and should you address it proactively?
It is almost certain that your prospects have questions they are not asking you. And they may be about you specifically. But they are asking these questions to themselves. The questions are as diverse as the number of salespeople and prospects. You should be able to guess what some of them are. Yet, in terms of behavioral finance, we see that many salespeople avoid the questions, even though they know the answers

could be fatal. Instead they tend to avoid the issue(s) and hope prospects will come up with an acceptable answer(s) and that the sales process can continue. This is rarely the case. What do we know about missing information? It typically raises negative assumptions and conclusions. An example from everyday life: when your car is in the repair shop and you hear nothing for a week, you speculate that the car is not being worked on, something horribly expensive was discovered that needs to be fixed, it's been stolen…all sorts of bad things. Usually, the truth is that there was a missed phone call or e-mail explaining the situation. Or, there was no update and the perceived situation is rapidly deteriorating.

7. Your competition is telling "true lies" about you, your product, and your company.

It's almost a certainty. What are "true lies?" They are bad things competitors (or even worse, your prospect) can say or think about you that sound completely plausible but in fact are untrue. Large firms all suffer the true lie that they are so big that your project or order will get lost and their great service reps will be reserved for big clients. Small firms are subject to true lies, too: their bench depth is so shallow that if something goes wrong, you're on your own. It's the "hit by a bus" syndrome. Sounds plausible, right? Address these true lies on your terms, not the competition's. In fact, always fight your battles on your terms. You should strive to select the time, battlefield, and your weapons of choice. If you do this regularly, it's hard to lose.

8. What are you—salesperson, client service rep, or practice leader?

How you answer this question will determine your future success. A key best practice is being focused on one of these three options. That is, the percentage of time spent on each of these three activities is highly correlated to the growth rate of the practice. I think you can guess that a higher percentage spent on sales activities was the number one best practice for growth.

But how much is enough? There was an inflection point in the data at 60 percent. That is, rapid growth occurred after the person was dedicating at least 60 percent of his/her time to business development. You can try to do it all, but it's only slowing your growth.

Lesson 6

● ● ●

Build Loyalty, Not Just a Book of Business

Of all the words you read in business books, perhaps none is more used and less understood than "loyalty." There are programs that want to make me loyal to Taco Bell and Starbucks and United Airlines. But is this real loyalty or just a pricing gimmick? Let's try to figure out what loyalty actually means and how you build it.

Loyalty

First, let's state the obvious: building a book of business = acquisition + retention. Retention is the loyalty element, the dark matter that holds together the universe of business. What is it exactly? I define it as the probability that the value stream flowing from a customer or client will continue into the future. OK, great. Sounds like a definition from a behavioral economist. But what does loyalty really mean to you?

Loyalty is *not* just buying more product because you keep dropping the price. Loyalty is *not* just staying with a provider because you are happy. Loyalty is best defined by what it "buys" you. Loyalty buys you certain things that are extremely valuable. What are they?

Advocacy

First, loyalty buys advocacy from your clients. You can spend millions on advertising and never receive the kind of impact delivered by a random collection of your users saying positive things about you. Loyalty also buys you forgiveness. If something goes dreadfully wrong, loyal customers will tell you about it, assume it was an aberration, and expect your performance will return to normal immediately. A disloyal client will walk away as soon as possible, usually without saying a thing. In the case of disloyal clients, the first symptom of a problem is sudden death. Still, even loyalty won't buy you forgiveness for a series of misadventures. Once a loyal client or customer sees that bad performance is the "new normal," it's time to abandon ship. But loyal clients will usually give you time to fix things.

Patience

Loyalty also buys you the client's patience. If a competitor launches a better product, the loyal client will assume you too will offer it soon. But like all relationships, there is a limit to such benevolence, and the loyalist eventually gives up in frustration and leaves.

Cross-selling

Loyalty also buys you easy cross-selling opportunities for other products you offer. A loyal customer is always willing to deepen a good relationship.

So how do you build loyalty, particularly in a commoditized product market? You start before you even have the relationship. Surprisingly, our data from many industries show that not all satisfied clients are highly loyal and not all loyal clients are highly satisfied. Satisfaction and loyalty are correlated, but it is not universally true that only highly satisfied clients are highly loyal. So there has to be something else. Once again, behavioral economics has an explanation.

Perhaps the most powerful loyalty building blocks are:

* Cultural selling
* Moving from economic norms to social norms
* Customer experience
* Collaboration
* Thought leadership

Keep in mind that there is no hierarchy here, but all of these building blocks are connected. Collectively, they build trust. They lead clients and prospects to trust you. And trust catalyzes the impact of each building block.

Cultural selling—the art of finding clients who want to be serviced in the way you want to service them—is a quick trip to Loyaltyville. It is. It may result in slower short-term growth but far greater and stable long-term growth. Most salespeople have never seen a prospect they didn't like. In their mind, every prospect's needs align perfectly with the capabilities of the salesperson's company. But if there isn't a cultural match, trouble will soon follow. The buyer feels betrayed. The seller feels exploited. Or even worse. Lawsuits appear. Brands are ruined.

Ask yourself: Do you and your prospect really have a cultural fit? Do you really want to work for these people? Will they turn out to be your worst nightmare? Commonly in business this conflict never has to be resolved by the salesperson because sales and client relationship management are separate functions. "Not my problem," says the salesperson as he/she walks away with a commission. Pray for this company and client.

When everybody's expectations are aligned, there are fewer disappointments, satisfaction soars, and loyalty abounds. JD Power studies, to use one example, focus on customer satisfaction. However, loyalty is the thing to strive for. Loyalty is bankable, satisfaction is not.

Moving from economic norms to social norms was described by Dr. Dan Ariely, a professor of psychology and behavioral economics at Duke, in his best-selling book *Predictably Irrational*. Here is how it works: the market norm is to have a linear transfer of value in one form to value in another form. For example, I can sell my valuable hours of time to an employer in exchange for wages, another form of value. The market clears. If I stop working, the transfer of value to me in the form of wages stops. And if the work conditions become intolerable, my hours may no longer be for sale to that employer. Not much loyalty there, but the rules are clear. If there is an emergency at night and my employer needs me to work, I ask for more wages.

A social norm means money cannot be exchanged for service. Dr. Ariely explains it with the following parable demonstrating how a social norm was violated:

> You are at your mother-in-law's house for Thanksgiving dinner, and what a sumptuous spread she has put on the table for you! The turkey is roasted to a golden brown; the stuffing is homemade and exactly the way you like it. Your kids are delighted: the sweet potatoes are crowned with marshmallows. And your wife is flattered: her favorite recipe for pumpkin pie has been chosen for dessert.
>
> The festivities continue into the late afternoon. You loosen your belt and sip a glass of wine. Gazing fondly across the table at your mother-in-law, you rise to your feet and pull out your wallet. "Mom, for all the love you've put into this, how much do I owe you?" you say sincerely. As silence descends on the gathering, you wave a handful of bills. "Do you think three hundred dollars will do it? No, wait, I should give you four hundred!"
>
> This is not a picture that Norman Rockwell would have painted. A glass of wine falls over; your mother-in-law stands up red-faced, your sister-in-law shoots you an angry look, and your niece bursts into tears. Next year's Thanksgiving celebration, it seems, may be a frozen dinner in front of the television set.

The point is that the mother-in-law did not prepare the meal under the dynamics of a market norm. She was functioning under the dynamics of a social norm through which value is not expressed monetarily or linearly. As Dr. Ariely said, "Social norms explain why we are happy to do things, but not when we are paid to do them."

If something needs to get done, people functioning under a social norm do whatever it takes to make it happen for free. Keeping your relationships functioning on a market norm never builds loyalty, and these relationships will collapse at the first sign of trouble. The point about giving away a free meatball in the form of white papers, free advice and counsel, and so on is a good example of functioning under a social norm. *And* it was established before there was a client relationship. Which world do you want to exist in?

Customer experience. Every product and service has at least two dimensions: physical and experiential. An automobile has weight, colors, smells, speed, gas mileage, and so on. A lawyer has a physical dimension: contracts to be signed, arguments on your behalf in court, and so on. These physical features are powerful drivers of customer satisfaction, but not nearly as powerful in driving loyalty. What is customer experience, and where does it occur? Simply put, customer experience is what it "feels" like to be a customer of your firm. This feeling exists in the right brain. If you are going to get inside your prospect's head, make sure you end up on the right side.

Collaboration—everybody is talking about it. Collaboration is the partnering of a buyer and seller to achieve a common goal. Does it ever really happen? Yes—among enlightened companies that focus on long-term gains, not short-term results. The problem is that the business world is becoming increasingly focused on short-term time horizons. "I gotta make my quarterly numbers or I am screwed." When collaboration truly happens, it is a thing of beauty. Outcomes unachievable by each party alone are realized together. Relationships are strengthened. Social norms are maximized. Loyalty soars.

Sadly, collaboration rarely happens because of economic constraints such as profit margins and time lines. Or, if physical examples are offered to reflect collaboration on the design of a house, it is unclear where the homeowner and architect contributed to the final product.

How can I tell you what you contributed to the final product? If collaboration truly happens, the two parties are often friends for life. They were on the same side of the desk seeking mutually beneficial goals, market norms were suspended, and social norms became the hallmark of the relationship.

Thought leadership. Another widely used and rarely understood concept is thought leadership. First, it is not necessarily the same thing as product innovation, although the two can go together. Thought leadership is about having the vision to stand on the shoulders of the marketplace and see a different picture, a bigger picture. It is almost always coming from the intuitive side of your brain. Many people confuse thought leadership with providing new information on a topic. Behavioral economists generally agree that to qualify as thought leadership an idea must make us think differently about a familiar topic (or create an entirely new topic) *and* make us behave differently. If it doesn't change behavior, information—no matter how new—is simply, well, information. What is the value of thought leadership to you and the prospect or client? I have spoken to roughly one thousand business decision makers about why they decided to seek a new provider. The answers range from bad service to the price/quality/value balance being out of kilter. Those are relatively easy to fix. But the most vexing yet promising is the concern that they were missing out on new solutions to old problems. They also were afraid that they were unaware of risks they faced or opportunities they were missing. Interestingly, the strength of the perception of thought leadership is highly correlated to very low intent to switch to another provider. If clients feel you are keeping them on the leading edge of the ideas marketplace, they are unlikely to leave you. Finally, keep in mind that thought leadership often is memorable. Breakthrough ideas are fascinating and stay in the audience's mind.

Because decisions to pick you are rarely made while you are still in the room, you want to leave the prospect with something to remember you by that differentiates you. Thought leadership will do it almost every time. It is amazing how many times we ask a prospect who just went through a vendor's presentation what his or her primary takeaway was about the proposal or company, and the answer is "nothing."

Let's look at some examples of thought leadership from across time to the current day:

* Copernicus: "Hey, you guys! The Earth revolves around the Sun—not the other way around!"
* Darwin: Evolution, not intelligent design
* Einstein: Time is relative
* USPS to e-mail
* Analog to digital
* Wired to wireless or iPhone

Part Two:
Transforming Your Role

Lesson 7

● ● ●

Sell Creative Outcomes

When I ask businesses, "What business are you really in?" the answers rarely capture the essence of the value their product or brand represents. Perfect example: let's consider an exciting, creative industry that deals in inspirational beauty such as landscape architecture. I was speaking to a group of landscape architects and heard the following when I asked, "What business are you in?" and "What are you really selling?":

"Our firm is committed to excellence and service, exceptional craftsmanship, imaginative use of materials, and our innovative horticultural palettes."

"Our firm sculpts and navigates space through a seamless integration of landscape architect, art, and architecture."

"We employ a rigorous design process to create thoughtful and meaningful landscapes with a sound theoretical base."

"We regard the design of outdoor space as both a technical and artistic expression that carefully balances the character of materials, architecture, and people within the historical, cultural, and environmental context."

"With an unyielding passion for design and its relationship to natural and man-made forms, we offer a progressive blend of landscape architecture, embracing utility while exploring contemporary relevance and innovation in outdoor planning."

"We offer a strong vision and meticulous attention to every detail from design through completion, creating elegant, timeless design solutions."

OK, not very inspiring, but that is how they describe themselves and what they do. Interestingly, they tend to see themselves in an empirical, linear way. But I won't be judgmental. Next I spoke to homeowners (actually more like owners of palatial mansions) who have hired a landscape architect, and I asked them why they used the ones they used. After all, every one of us can put plants in the ground and water them. So it must be something beyond the labor involved. Here is a sampling of what they said:

"I wanted to capture the feelings I had when I was a kid walking through the woods around our farm."

"I write for a living and wanted to be surrounded by an environment that frees up my mind to go to that place where I can find new ideas and dimensions."

"I want the landscape to express who I am as a person, how I want people to think about me."

"I love nature. I want the beauty of nature around me."

You see the difference? All the clients were seeking creative outcomes. Outcomes that take them to a beautiful, inspiring place they need/want to be. Outcomes that express to them and those around them what kind of people they are or want others to think they are. These users of landscape architecture couldn't care less about the things the architects think they are selling. They couldn't care less about the technical process to get them there. Ultimately, they want to feel good about themselves, and perhaps more importantly, they want others to think highly of them (although they hope it is painless and not astronomically expensive).

Take wealth managers as another example. They view themselves as experts who offer a long list of technical financial analyses and complicated products wrapped in a process of data gathering to produce something called "optimization." The wealthy prospects and clients are looking for a safe, secure sense of the future for themselves and their loved ones. They essentially want to never worry about money and managing it ever again. The clients don't want to buy the process or the technology. They don't even understand it or want to understand it. They made their money by designing electronic devices, practicing medicine, or selling vintage cars. It is not their job to understand what the wealth manger does or how he/she does it. Wealth managers are selling linear products and processes to people who are looking for emotional outcomes. The wealthy want to worry the least about the thing of which they have the most.

Keep in mind who is benefiting from what you sell. Remember, I said that...

> **KEY TAKEAWAY:** *People don't pay for the features and process; they buy benefits. Ultimately, people will buy what you sell if it leaves them somehow better off after they consume it. And creative, intuitive thinking often fetches a higher price than left-brained thinking.*

Finally, ask yourself this question when pondering what you are selling: "Am I simply promising *not* to behave poorly?" Examples abound from leading international companies. Here are a few:

We will never let you stand in line more than three minutes.

We will sit down with you to ask you questions in order to create a personalized wealth-management strategy.

We believe in collaborating with you, *the client.*

Knowing what you are selling and what business you are really in, alone, is critical. Let's apply this concept to examples of enormous real-world successes in the next chapter. We all love success stories. Keep reading…here they come.

Lesson 8

•   •   •

Pair Your Product and Brand Personality

The dynamics at work in the concepts laid out in the last chapter can be explained with a relatively new idea: product and brand personality. Understanding product and brand personality is a huge advantage. To explain it, I will use the examples of Rolex watches and Apple iPhones. But first some behavioral economics theory. Don't worry; it's fun theory! In 2008, one of our professors in the RAND Behavioral Finance Forum, Dr. Meir Statman of Santa Clara University, introduced a groundbreaking concept he called brand and product personality. Here is how it works: Every product is paired with a brand, so one without the other usually results in a commercial disaster. Interestingly, the product can be a physical widget, a service, *and* it can be you. You are selling yourself to someone else every day. You may be an adviser, an agent, a production worker, an artist, or a white-, blue-, or pink-collar worker. Product and brand personality applies to all of us who want to be in professional relationships with other human beings…almost all of us want to exchange economic or social value.

Every—and I really mean every—brand/product pairing has three dimensions:

Utilitarian: What the product or service actually does

Emotive: How the product or service *makes others perceive you* because you use that product/brand pairing

Emotional: How the product or service *makes you perceive yourself* because you use that product/brand pairing

Let's start with the example of Rolex versus Timex. One new Rolex retails for US$19,000. A new Timex Men's Metal Analog and Digital Combo Watch retails for US $50. Now, the analysis:

Utilitarian: What the product or service actually does

Both products do exactly the same thing. They tell you the relative positions of the earth and sun from where you are standing at any moment. Interestingly, the two watches are considered to be equal in this dimension, so it's a draw on "utilitarian." Yet there has to be a reason why intelligent people will pay 380 times the price to get the same product. Let's move on to the next level of analysis.

Emotive: How the product or service makes others perceive you because you use that product/brand pairing

Here is where the pairings start to depart. If you ask one hundred people what attributes they would ascribe to Rolex owners and what attributes they would ascribe to Timex owners, you will get two distinct profiles. But even more important is what the Rolex owner *thinks* the attributes are that people would ascribe to Rolex owners versus Timex owners. Well, how do Rolex owners develop that opinion? A lot of ways, but just look at the Rolex brochures to see what they are really selling and what business they are actually in. The brochures are dense with images of successful, intelligent, thought-leading, inquisitive, envelope-pushing, international, discerning, wealthy, attractive, healthy, active, physically fit, exclusive, sought-after people. They even have what they call "The World of Rolex," which consists of nations called:

* Equestrian
* Golf
* The Arts
* Skiing
* Exploration
* Golf
* Tennis
* Yachting
* Motor sports

Are we still talking about knowing the relative positions of the earth and sun from where you are standing at any moment? In my mind, it is well worth it to have people think all these things about me without having to accomplish more than writing a check for $19,000. How is that for a fast track to success?

Now let's look at the Timex marketing campaign: product and feature dense, and prices everywhere. At best, they show that they advertise in fitness magazines. People may think that you are not affected by brand names, don't care to show off your purchasing power, have other things to demonstrate what kind of person you are, and so on. But for the people who buy the Rolex, they likely think it says you are poor, even though many Timex owners could probably come up with the $19,000 if they needed to.

Emotional: How the product or service makes you perceive yourself because you use that product/brand pairing

Having looked at the emotive dimension, it is not hard to imagine what the emotional dimension may do for the Rolex owner. Many want to not just think but actually *believe* they are successful, intelligent, thought-leading, inquisitive, envelope-pushing, international, discerning, wealthy, attractive, healthy, active, physically fit, exclusive, sought-after people.

Of course, both Rolex and Timex sell a lot of watches. It's a matter of market research to identify and measure the capacity of both market segments. There are likely many people in the Timex target market who want what a

Rolex can deliver. Imagine the impact on Rolex owners' self-perceptions if Rolex came out with a product priced for the Timex market. Imagine the failure if Timex came out with a watch priced for the Rolex market. I guess this explains why you never see Timex knockoffs for sale on the sidewalks of Manhattan, but the Rolex knockoffs are everywhere. Imagine Rolex self-perceptions at Timex prices! What a country! It may be impolite to tell people what you earn, but people sure do love to hint at it!

Ponder another quick example: the iPhone. It was product and brand personality that took a collection of not particularly leading-edge technologies and packaged and branded them in such a way that iPhones became a phenomenon so powerful that people actually started to self-identify as "Apple iPhone people." When someone opens an Apple laptop in a meeting, it changes people's perception of that person—positively and negatively.

So are you selling your products at the utilitarian level? Even more importantly, are you selling yourself at the utilitarian level? Chances are very high you are. What does using your product and brand—or *you*—say about the world to your customers? How does it make them feel about themselves? If you don't have an answer, or worse, if your answer is "nothing!" you may have taken the advantage represented by product and brand personality and given it away.

Now let's see what you think is your product and brand personality. Answer the following questions to find the answer:

I/my product does the following things: _____

_____

_____

_____

As a result of being associated with me/my product, people think the following things about my clients:

_____

_____

_____

_____

As a result of being associated with my brand, people think the following things about my clients:

_____

_____

_____

_____

As a result of being associated with my product, my clients think the following things about themselves:

_____

_____

_____

_____

Lesson 9

● ● ●

Be Ruthless in Assessing Your Uniqueness

Can a new product be that advantage you're looking for, and if so, for how long? Let's take a hard, maybe painful look at your products. While consulting for major corporations over the years, I have found that they often become emotionally attached to their products. Just look at what happened with Mattel and Barbie and Ken. These dolls actually came alive in their minds. And that can be a good thing as long as it doesn't cloud your judgment. Admitting your child is not very good looking or smart or useful is painful for a parent. Doing the same thing regarding a product is equally painful. But it might be necessary.

First of all, let's ask the heretical question: "Is it necessary to innovate, or is it better to copy others' innovation?" By looking at the world economy, you can see an enormous amount of innovation going on. But you also see a world of commoditized products. Innovative products are being commoditized often within months of their market introduction. Think about your industry: What innovations in the past ten years have substantially and permanently changed market share? Surely your industry has innovated, but was that to the advantage of the end users or your company?

Now let's take a look at your products on the drawing board. Are they innovative, and if so, are they going to capture sustainable advantages in terms of more market share, greater profits, greater stability, and so on? In my thirty years of product concept testing, the answer is almost always no. I'll explain. When I test products or product concepts for innovativeness and their likely effect on the company, I often employ Kano analysis. This analysis was developed by Noriaki Kano, professor emeritus at Tokyo University of Science. Professor Kano is an educator, lecturer, writer, and consultant in the field of quality management. He is the developer of a customer-satisfaction model (now known as the Kano model) whose simple ranking scheme distinguishes between essential and differentiating attributes related to concepts of customer quality. If your company adheres to the Six Sigma program and you have a black belt, you have been exposed to this technique. It can be applied to products, services, advertising messaging, and even to you as a person, salesperson, adviser, agent, and so on.

The technique is simple but extremely powerful because it makes companies know if they should proceed with development or put down the Kool-Aid and start thinking about another way to spend their R&D dollars. To conduct the analysis, you simply ask the development group, marketing team, sales team (or yourself) to list the salient features of the concept under scrutiny. I will spare you the details, but essentially each feature is categorized in terms of its impact on the probability of selling the entire concept against the competition. The interesting feature of Kano analysis is you ask the probability question if the feature exists and then if it doesn't exist.

Let's use an automobile as the example. Looking at the table below, the features of the automobile on the drawing board are listed down the side, and the chances of beating the competition are across the top.

	Effect on Chances of Beating the Competition if Feature is "In" or "Not in" the Design	
Features	**In the Design**	**Not in the Design**
Brakes	No increase in chances	Chances reduced to zero
GPS Standard	No increase in chances	No change in chances
High Mileage	Increase in chance as feature increases	Decrease in chance as feature decreases
Nonpolluting	Increase in chance as feature increases	Decrease in chance as feature decreases
Makes you cool	Huge increase in chances	No change in chances
Hydrogen Fuel	Huge increase in chances	No change in chances

What have we learned? Features such as brakes are what Professor Kano described as "must be." Without them you don't even have a car. GPS doesn't change the chances the automobile will beat the competition whether it is included or not. He refers to this type of feature as "indifferent." Mileage and level of pollution are referred to as a "continuous" features; the more you have of those features, the better the chances of beating the competition and vice versa. These are often referred to as "comparison shopping" features. And, finally, "makes you cool" and hydrogen fuel make the sale almost certain if they are in the design, yet have no impact on the chance of beating the competition if they are not in the design. These are called "surprise and delight" features. The problem with these "surprise and delight" features is they quickly devolve into "must be" features as the competition, sensing a threat, develops the same features. Look where GPS is now and where it was twenty years ago.

The point is that you need to be ruthlessly honest in assessing the uniqueness of your products and decide if you have an attractive or ugly child. My experience is that the analysis leads to either major redesign or abandonment of the development project. Imagine doing this analysis on yourself. Very intriguing results always ensue. But if you embody the product, such as with an adviser, agent, broker, architect, lawyer, writer, actor, athlete, and so on, you really need to be Kano'ed. The same is particularly true if you are a salesperson. The other point: while products can be the advantage you need, you can't rely on that advantage being a superior weapon for long. Competitive market forces will see to that.

Lesson 10

●　●　●

Avoid Commoditizing Yourself

Thinking about the downside of competitive market forces, what can be an enduring advantage for you? An enduring point of differentiation? Every product has three dimensions: physical, brand, and experiential. We have posited that product differentiation as a growth strategy will almost always fall short in the long run. So let's look at brand. What is brand? It is the promise you make to the market. Is your promise unique? Specific? Compelling? Simply a promise to not behave poorly? Brands vary widely on awareness. However, they tend to be undifferentiated. That is, they don't really stand out as having a unique meaning or promise as compared to competitors.

I have seen this firsthand. In the analysis I ask my clients (whose job it is to know their market and their competitors' positioning and brands) to give me the names of their eight strongest competitors. I then analyze their marketing materials in brochures, websites, advertising, and so on. Now, let me address something you are probably thinking: websites and brochures never close a deal, but they do reflect how providers view themselves and their prospects, what they believe are their strengths, and what unmet needs exist. I use their own words from the marketing materials and align the eight competitors' materials side by side on a board. I also include my clients' positioning and branding materials with the others. None of the materials are labeled with the competitor name they represent. I then ask the marketing group to identify the competitor that goes with each set of materials. Few of my clients have been able to reach consensus on which competitor goes with which set of materials. And, at best, nobody in the group could correctly identify more than two of the eight competitors. Few were able to identify their own branding.

This is profound! These companies paid millions to develop the brand and even more to promote it!

Let's perform another Kano analysis, this time on an adviser's brand using a real-world example.

Features	Effect on Chances of Beating the Competition if Feature is "In" or "Not in" the Design	
	In the Design	**Not in the Design**
Mission: To guide our clients with exceptional clarity as they work through the increasing volatility and complexities in the financial markets.	No change up or down (everyone says essentially the same thing).	No change up or down (they wouldn't be talking to you if they didn't already assume this were true; it is a table-stake feature).
Values: Our firm was built on the premise that investors are best served by advisers who are motivated to focus exclusively on the best interests of their clients.	No change up or down (sounds good, but it's just a promise to not behave poorly).	No change up or down (again, they wouldn't be talking to you if they didn't already assume this was true).
Philosophy: Advisory firms are only as strong as the people who create the advice.	No change up or down (obvious and nothing new).	No change up or down.
Functionality: Our services are designed to help you grow and protect your financial assets.	No change up or down (no comment necessary).	No change up or down (again, no comment necessary).

Branding in this case has done virtually nothing to increase the chances of being selected over a competitor, if, in fact, the prospect were comparison shopping. And if not, the brand promises simply define what an adviser does with no points of differentiation.

Another related point: neutralizing your competitive brand advantage is even easier than neutralizing competitive product advantages. With brand there is no physical evidence of the veracity of the promise. Anybody can say anything they want about their own brand, and the prospect, who is unaware of the company, has no idea if it's true or false. Your hard-earned competitive advantage is immediately eliminated with a competitor's simple, unsubstantiated claim. Consequently, you must be looking for defendable and important brand promises (i.e., claims) that are unique to your firm. If you can't think of any, create some.

The final frontier in the quest for differentiation is customer experience. The way it feels to do business and interact with you. As mentioned above, customer experience is a powerful driver of loyalty. For a client to get a great product from you, it shouldn't have to hurt. Automobiles have a customer experience through the service department, or the fact that they rarely need service.

To bring all these concepts together, let's think about the Apple iPhone.

The company took undifferentiated technology, wrapped in a brand that creates a self-identity ("I am an Apple person"), combined it with an unmatched customer experience, and built an empire. In the final analysis, you will want to assess if you are differentiated on any level in the prospect's mind. Be careful that the differentiation doesn't only exist in *your* mind. One last point on differentiation, which is the acid test on how well you did in escaping the curse of commoditization. Be honest in your answer:

If the world woke up tomorrow and you or your firm didn't exist anymore, what would the world be missing?

If you are having trouble coming up with answers, you are not alone. If you can figure this out, you're holding a large advantage.

Lesson 11

● ● ●

Make It Easy for Prospects to Make a Decision

Endless research has been performed by behavioral and neural economists and other scary-smart people on the subject of how decisions are made. Here are a few important concepts to know that you can apply at a practical level. First, the human brain seeks simplifying strategies when faced with complex decisions. Your job is to help people simplify the decision. Too much choice and information actually causes the brain to shut down and not make any decision at all. In her landmark research, Dr. Sheena Iyengar, a professor of business at Columbia University, conducted a behavioral economics study on decision making. She arranged thirty different jars of jam on a table at a country fair. She observed that many people stopped to look at the intriguing display, but virtually none actually purchased jam. In the next phase of her research, she displayed only six jars but found that sales were terrific. She applied this behavioral concept to workers' decision making about their workplace 401(k) savings plans. Her research found that as the number of investment options offered by the plan increased, participation in the plan declined significantly. Are you making the decision more complex, or are you helping the prospect simplify the decision (hopefully in your favor)?

The process of making a purchase decision requires collecting and analyzing a lot of data and information. But this analysis only reduces the number of candidates to consider by throwing out the weaker ones that obviously were not a good match. Now comes the hard part. The empirical brain must process and organize the information and transfer it to the intuitive side of the brain in order to create a safe, secure, feel-good decision. Interestingly, marketers tend to stop communicating their information at the empirical side. The smart marketer helps the decision maker transfer the information to the creative side of the brain and tells the brain what to intuit. At the end of the sales process, you must sum up all the information you provided and tell the decision maker what you stand for, what to remember about you, what virtues you represent, and what it will feel like after they select you. They want to make an intuited decision based on benefits and feel, not features. Make sure that happens in your case. Let your competitors wallow in the commoditizing, empirical-brained details while you compete in a different dimension. Otherwise, the decision maker will go into brain lock and make an empirically based decision based on spread-sheeted feature information.

Lesson 12

●　●　●

Take Control (of the Finals Meetings)

It is shocking how often sellers begin a finals presentation with information about themselves. They are exhausting precious minutes and decision makers' attention spans on things the buyers already should have been told. If you have to tell the decision makers the number of years you have been in business or the countries where you operate at this point, you have already failed. In finals meetings, you need to be telling them things about themselves. You need to be telling them how you will productively fit into their world, not how they will fit into your world. This is your moment to shine, to reduce the risk of picking you, and to increase the possible regret of not picking you. Sum up your argument, what you uniquely represent. I would rather lose because I didn't stand for the right thing than because they couldn't remember who I was.

> **KEY TAKEAWAY:** *Describe how their lives will be better for making a decision to pick you. You should have already told them how you will do it in previous meetings. Your goal is to build chemistry, move to social norms, add value that justifies your price, and demonstrate your partnering skills. And always finish strong.*

Dr. Daniel Kahneman, professor of psychology, emeritus, and professor of psychology and public affairs, emeritus, at Princeton University is considered the father of behavioral economics. He won the Nobel Prize for his work on decision making. His research revealed many things about us. One thing he revealed is that we have an experiencing self and a remembering self. He stated that our experiencing self "experiences" events (such as a finals presentation, for example) in very short intervals—three to four seconds—and then moves on to the next experience within the same event. It is the last few experiences that the remembering self will, well, *remember* about the event. The last few experiences will have the strongest effect on the perception of the entire event. So finish strong; tell the buyer what you want them to remember about you.

See Daniel Kahneman at TED 2010

http://www.ted.com/talks/daniel_kahneman_the_riddle_of_experience_vs_memory.html

Summary: *Using examples from vacations to colonoscopies, Nobel laureate and founder of behavioral economics Daniel Kahneman reveals how our "experiencing selves" and our "remembering selves" perceive happiness differently. This new insight has profound implications for economics, public policy, and our own self-awareness.*

And be sure it is a message that sticks. The decision makers are not going to decide the minute you finish your presentation. There will be a long delay before they have to compare you with your competitors to make a decision.

KEY TAKEAWAY: Having a message that persists, changes the way people think, and changes behavior is your biggest advantage!

About the Author

Warren Cormier is founder and president of Boston Research Technologies and is a noted researcher on behavior, specializing in behavioral economics. He has more than thirty-five years of quantitative and qualitative experience in financial-services research and strategic planning for the nation's largest financial institutions, banks, investment firms, insurance companies, mutual-fund companies, and brokerage firms.

Mr. Cormier, who is also Executive Director of the DCIIA Retirement Research Center, is recognized as a market-research leader in the defined contribution (DC) industry. He was voted by DC professionals as one of the "Top Twenty Most Influential People in the 401(k) Industry." He is the author of key studies that have become the standard for service quality and trend measurement in the 401(k) arena. He has also created similar studies for the adviser and participant channels as well as the highly successful DCP Institute, which brings together hundreds of retirement advisers, broker/dealers, asset managers, and DC plan providers to network and share creative ideas on practice building and servicing plan sponsors and participants.

In 2006, he cofounded the Behavioral Finance Forum with Dr. Shlomo Benartzi, chairman of the Consumer Decision Department and professor and cochair, Behavioral Decision-Making Group, UCLA/Anderson School of Management. The forum's mission is to foster collaboration between the world's leading behavioral finance academics and leading financial institutions to help consumers make better financial decisions.

Mr. Cormier has been quoted by Reuters and *Money* magazine, has appeared on C-SPAN, and is frequently interviewed by financial trade publications (including online). He has been an invited speaker on trends and the future of the investment industry at national industry conferences organized by the following:

*   ICI (Investment Company Institute)
*   AEI (American Enterprise Institute)

*   Society of Professional Administrators and Recordkeepers (SPARK), the largest professional society and lobbying group for the providers of 401(k) plans.
*   Pension & Investments
*   Mid-Sized Pension Conference
*   Profit Sharing Council of America

Mr. Cormier's interest in the arts has also contributed to his work. For about five years he owned a theater in Boston, serving as executive director, stage manager, and an actor in productions ranging from Shakespeare to experimental works, balancing his "left-brain" work in economics and sociology with arts projects that delve into human behavior from a "right-brain" perspective. He has served as president of the Board of Directors of the Z-Space Center for the Performing Arts in San Francisco.

A Boston-area native, he maintains offices in Boston and divides his time between Charlotte and San Francisco. Finally, he is a partner in Piccino, an Italian restaurant and café specializing in the cuisine of Lucca, located in the Dogpatch neighborhood of San Francisco.

Rugged Gold Miners

Jeff Savage

E **Enslow Publishers, Inc.**
40 Industrial Road
Box 398
Berkeley Heights, NJ 07922
USA

Original edition published as *Gold Miners of the Wild West* in 1995.

Library of Congress Cataloging-in-Publication Data
Savage, Jeff, 1961–
  Rugged gold miners : true tales of the Wild West / Jeff Savage.
    p. cm. — (True tales of the Wild West)
  Rev. ed. of: Gold miners of the Wild West. Springfield, N.J. : Enslow, c1995.
  Includes bibliographical references and index.
  Summary: "Examines gold miners, including the discovery of gold in the United States, the
California Gold Rush, the daily lives of miners and prospectors, and how the rush for gold
changed the landscape of America"—Provided by publisher.
  ISBN 978-0-7660-4020-5
  1. Gold miners—West (U.S.)—History—19th century—Juvenile literature. 2. West (U.S.)—
Gold discoveries—Juvenile literature. I. Savage, Jeff, 1961– Gold miners of the Wild West. II.
Title.
  F591.S327 2012
  978'.02—dc23
                            2011026343

Printed in the United States of America

Paperback ISBN 978-1-4644-0028-5

ePUB ISBN 978-1-4645-0480-8

PDF ISBN 978-1-4646-0480-5

092011 Lake Book Manufacturing, Inc., Melrose Park, IL

10 9 8 7 6 5 4 3 2 1

To Our Readers: We have done our best to make sure all Internet addresses in this book were
active and appropriate when we went to press. However, the author and the Publisher have no
control over, and assume no liability for, the material available on those Internet sites or on other
Web sites they may link to. Any comments or suggestions can be sent by e-mail to comments@
enslow.com or to the address on the back cover.

Enslow Publishers, Inc., is committed to printing our books on recycled paper. The paper
in every book contains 10% to 30% post-consumer waste (PCW). The cover board on the
outside of each book contains 100% PCW. Our goal is to do our part to help young people
and the environment too!

Illustration Credits: Enslow Publishers, Inc., p. 23; © Enslow Publishers, Inc. / Paul Daly,
p. 1; Courtesy Everett Collection, p. 10; The Granger Collection, NYC, pp. 14, 43; Library of
Congress Prints and Photographs, pp. 6, 25, 31, 33, 37; © 2011 Photos.com, a division of
Getty Images, p. 17.

Cover Illustration: © Enslow Publishers, Inc. / Paul Daly.

Contents

chapter 1

A Golden Discovery

James Marshall strolled about, breathing in the frigid air, inspecting the grounds, as he did every Monday morning. The men on his crew prepared for another hectic workweek. They were building John A. Sutter's water-driven sawmill.

About fourteen thousand United States citizens lived in California at the time. On January 24, 1848, something was about to happen in the sleepy town of Coloma that would change everything.

Marshall examined the newly built tailrace, the small canal that discharged the water leaving the mill. Three days earlier, the workmen had dammed the south fork of the American River in order to direct a flow of water through the mill. Marshall saw that the tailrace was working well.

James Marshall is pictured standing in front of John Sutter's sawmill in Coloma, California, where he discovered gold.

That was not all he saw. The river had swept away rock and rubble, leaving silt in part of the tailrace. Marshall glanced up at the dam, then back at the sawmill and tailrace. Looking closely at the silt and noticing something shining in the early morning sun, he wondered if he could be seeing things. He squinted as he looked even closer at the silt. The dirt sparkled.

Marshall scraped up some of the silt in his hand and rubbed it with his fingers. Shiny flakes and small nuggets separated from the dirt.

For years, Marshall had heard rumors about gold in the foothills of the Sierra Nevada mountain range. Could this be gold? He bent over and gathered up more silt. More small gold nuggets appeared. James Marshall was an excitable man to begin with. On this morning, his heart was pounding. He grabbed a rock and hammered a nugget with it. The gleaming metal flattened easily, as gold should. Fool's gold, which looks like real gold but is worthless, would have broken into bits. Marshall was sure now that he had discovered gold!

For two days, Marshall wondered what to do. Should he tell the workmen? What if they killed him and hoarded all the gold? Should he keep the secret to himself? How would he be able to concentrate on building the sawmill? Finally, he decided to tell his boss, John Sutter.

Marshall rode forty-five miles to Sutter's Fort, arriving there on January 28. He was sweating from excitement as he burst into Sutter's office.

"He told me he had something of the utmost importance to tell me," Sutter wrote in his diary, "that he wanted to speak to me in private, and begged me to take him to some isolated place where no one could possibly overhear us."[1]

Sutter and his bookkeeper were alone in the house. Marshall insisted on going upstairs with his boss, and Sutter obliged. The two men entered a private room. Marshall began to tell of his discovery. He took a piece of cloth from his pocket and began unfolding it. Suddenly, the bookkeeper walked in to ask Sutter a question.

"My God, didn't I tell you to lock the door?" Marshall yelled.[2] Sutter sent the bookkeeper out and then convinced Marshall that the bookkeeper had no idea what was going on. Marshall took no chances. He bolted the door and then pushed a wardrobe against it. Then he removed from the cloth a few of the gold nuggets that he had discovered at the mill. Sutter looked closely at a nugget. "Well, it looks like gold," Sutter said. "Let us test it."[3]

The two men looked in Sutter's encyclopedia for some of the different ways to test gold. They pounded the nuggets and weighed them in water. They dipped them in nitric acid to see if they resisted corrosion; Gold would not come apart in the strong, toxic acid.

The nuggets passed all the tests. Marshall definitely had found gold.

Marshall returned to Sutter's Mill, where he told the workmen about his discovery. At first, they were not excited. They continued to build the mill and only dug for gold on Sunday—their day off. When the mill was finished, some of the men began to spend all their time prospecting for gold. The news spread to San Francisco and eventually to the East Coast. Most people did not believe that gold had been discovered. They thought it was a trick to get people to settle in California.

Reports continued to be published. A letter was printed in the November 1848 issue of the *American Journal of Science and Arts*. The last paragraph read: "Gold has been found recently on the Sacramento, near Sutter's Fort. It occurs in small masses in the sands of a new millrace, and is said to promise well."[4] Still, most of the eight hundred people who lived in San Francisco didn't react.

Then one day, a man named Samuel Brannan got people excited. Brannan lived a few miles below Sutter's Fort, and he had opened a supply store for miners. Not many customers came. So, Brannan filled a bottle with gold dust and rode to San Francisco.

He walked up and down the streets, held the bottle of gold dust high over his head, and shouted, "Gold, gold! Gold from the American River!"[5] Before long, fewer than a hundred people were left in San Francisco. The rest were digging for gold near Sutter's Mill. First, of course, they stopped for supplies at Sam Brannan's store.

A view of San Francisco in 1851. After gold was discovered, many people left San Francisco to go to Sutter's sawmill in search of gold.

Easterners began taking this gold talk seriously. Wild tales were being spread, first of nuggets of gold, then boulders of gold, then mountains of gold, and rivers gleaming with gold. The rush was on!

John Sutter was disappointed that gold was on his property. He owned thousands of acres of land that he named Nueva Helvetia (*Helvetia* is the Latin name for Switzerland, the land of his ancestors) and filled it with horses, cattle, mules, sheep, and hogs. Sutter just wanted to manage his land and watch his herds increase. For him, this gold rush could spoil everything.

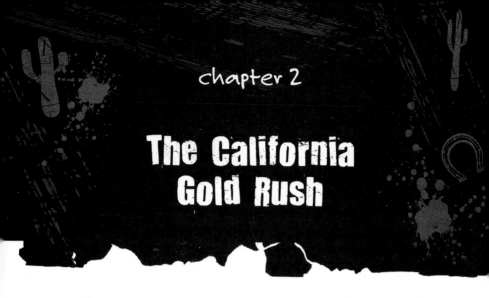

chapter 2

The California Gold Rush

The gold "discovery" of 1848 came as no surprise to some. American Indians probably knew for centuries about gold in the area, but they had no use for it. Mexican authorities used it in small quantities for jewelry and decorations. Yankee traders from the East would take home tiny nuggets or flakes, mainly as souvenirs. The American Indians and Mexicans also knew that news of a gold rush would lure thousands of white settlers.

In fact, gold had been mined in California some years earlier. Francisco Lopez, a Mexican cattle rancher, discovered gold northwest of Los Angeles, in the San Fernando Valley, on March 9, 1842. Lopez was returning home that day from tending his cattle in Placerita Canyon. On the way home, he remembered to pick some wild onions for his wife. As he pulled the onions out of the ground, Lopez noticed that shiny particles were attached to the onion roots. He had found gold! A local gold rush followed, and the land was worked over.

Getting There

Thousands of United States citizens packed their belongings and set out for California in 1848. Emigrants living in New York, Massachusetts, and other states along the East Coast had a choice of routes. Many sailed south on clipper ships to South America, around Cape Horn, and up the Pacific Ocean to San Francisco Bay. It was a long and expensive journey, but it was not as physically demanding as other routes.

Others traveled south by boat to Panama. There they crossed the Isthmus of Panama on foot. Hiking across the Central American country in the oppressive heat was difficult. Reaching the Pacific Ocean, they sailed north to California.

Emigrants from the Midwest took the overland route. The most common route, and certainly the cruelest, was the overland route. There were northerly trails, southerly trails, and rugged paths over the Sierra. It was hot and dusty in the summer and then

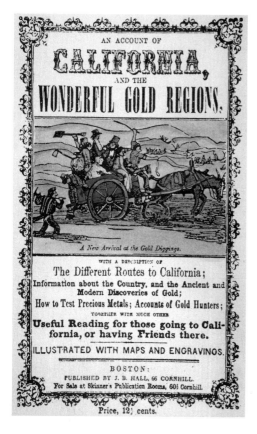

AN ACCOUNT OF

CALIFORNIA,

AND THE

WONDERFUL GOLD REGIONS.

A New Arrival at the Gold Diggings.

WITH A DESCRIPTION OF

The Different Routes to California;

Information about the Country, and the Ancient and Modern Discoveries of Gold;

How to Test Precious Metals; Accounts of Gold Hunters;

TOGETHER WITH MUCH OTHER

Useful Reading for those going to California, or having Friends there.

ILLUSTRATED WITH MAPS AND ENGRAVINGS.

BOSTON:
PUBLISHED BY J. B. HALL, 66 CORNHILL.
For Sale at Skinner's Publication Rooms, 60½ Cornhill.

Price, 12½ cents.

Word began to spread across the United States about gold in California. Americans on the East Coast had to figure out the best route to the West Coast. This is the cover of a guide to the "gold regions" of California printed in Boston, Massachusetts, in 1849. The guide provided routes to California, methods to test precious metals, and other maps and illustrations.

cold and wet as winter arrived. Along the route, food was difficult to come by. Clean water often was scarce. Wagon trains broke down. Horses died. Emigrants crossing American Indian territory were considered intruders and were attacked. The trails were littered with tragedy.

For safety, travelers were advised to go west across America in groups that included at least four grown men. In one popular guidebook, author D. C. Oakes wrote that six months on the trail required, among other things, twenty-five pounds of gunpowder and fifty pounds of lead (for bullets).

John Goller

John Goller, a prospector from Illinois, traveled to California in 1849 with a group of other miners. Goller's group decided to avoid the colder northerly routes. They would cross Death Valley to the south. It was a bad idea. For fifty-two agonizing days, Goller's party struggled to cross the hot, barren wilderness. They went for days without food or water. One man died, and another went crazy and wandered away.

When the survivors finally made it to civilization, Goller had with him a handful of gold nuggets. He had found them somewhere in Death Valley, but he could not be certain where the mine was. Instead of going north, Goller decided to stay in Los Angeles. He spent the rest of his life leading expeditions in search of the lost mine. He never found it.

All through 1849, as people arrived in the Golden State, they were met by thousands more who poured in from Asia, South America, and Europe. These masses of gold prospectors became known as the Forty-Niners.

The Miners

Miners came from everywhere. Their backgrounds were as varied as the land in which they dug. Before trying their luck at prospecting, they might have been doctors, lawyers, editors, or lawmen. One writer said, "All mixed together you had shrewd New England business-men, rollicking sailors, Australian convicts and cut-throats, Mexican and frontier desperadoes, hardy backwoodsmen, professional gamblers, whiskey-dealers, general swindlers . . . professional miners from all parts of the world."[1]

Chinese immigrants poured into California in the 1850s in search of gold strikes. Although they were eager to find gold in what they called the Gold Mountain, they suffered from race discrimination at the hands of white settlers. The Chinese were prohibited from working the best mines, yet they proved industrious by squeezing out the remaining gold from old diggings. In many communities, they worked for very low wages as cooks or laundrymen.

Staking a Claim

Prospectors could not just dig anywhere they wanted. They had to make a claim on an area of land. If no one else had filed a claim on this piece of land, it could be claimed by the prospector. Nobody was permitted to search for gold on another person's claim. Those who did were called claim-jumpers. Sometimes, they were shot by claim owners.

James Marshall, the man who discovered the gold at Sutter's Mill, was forced by a gang of miners to leave his own claim. Even John Sutter, on whose land

Gold miners working in California use a sluice to filter out the gold from the rocky and sandy soil at the bottom of a stream.

the gold had been discovered, lost out. His land was grabbed, and he spent a fortune in legal fees trying to reclaim it.

Getting the Gold

Would-be prospectors had much to learn about mining. They couldn't just stroll along gathering gold nuggets. There were several methods used for digging gold.

The simplest method, panning, was used around rivers and creeks. Panning required a tin pan about three or four inches deep and a foot or so wide. Gravel was scooped into the pan, water was added, and the pan was skillfully swirled. Because gold is heavier than dirt, the silt spilled out of the pan, and the gold remained in the pan. This gold on the surface of creek beds was called placer gold.

When the placer gold along rivers and creeks had been removed, miners began to use larger equipment. Cradles and long toms were contraptions that separated the gold from the mud. They were flat wooden troughs, sometimes thirty feet or more in length, that stretched along the river. Mud was shoveled into the troughs and then was washed from one end to the other. A screen or a series of ridges were built into the top end of each trough. They held the heaviest material, the gold, while the dirt washed away. Because these tools were costly to build, mining began to get expensive. People formed partnerships to share the cost.

Some miners eager to dig were too poor to buy even the simplest tools. That is where grubstaking came in. A backer would outfit the miners with needed tools and supply them with food in return for a share of whatever they found.

H.A.W. Tabor was one such grubstaker. Tabor gave seventeen dollars to two prospectors in Leadville in the Colorado Territory. A year later, they presented him with his share of their find—a million dollars. However, Tabor made that money from silver, not gold. Most grubstakers, like most miners, never found the riches they were looking for.

Mining was not only a grueling business; it was hazardous as well. Miners had to be wary of claim-jumpers and bandits. It was hard to survive in bad weather. As prospecting became more elaborate and mines were built, one out of every three men who worked in a mine for at least a decade suffered a serious injury; one out of eight got killed. An estimated 7,500 men died in mines, and another 20,000 were badly wounded.

Mining Camps

There was plenty of gold in California. Nearly $600 million in gold was mined from the ground by 1860. Another $700 million was found between 1860 and 1900. Most of the placer gold, however, was skimmed away within the first year.

By the end of 1850, only one in a hundred panners made a decent profit at mining. The names of the mining camps reveal their disappointment and despair. Among the camps and diggings were Poverty Flat, Dry Diggings, Bed Bug, Drytown, Mad Mule Gulch, Git-up-and-Git, Loafer Hill, Murderer's Bar, and Rough and Ready.

By 1866, there were more than one thousand mining camps in the West. They varied in size and shape, usually depending on the amount of gold nearby. One observer described them this way:

> The typical camp of the gold prime of '49 was flush, reckless, flourishing, and vigorous. Saloons and gambling-houses abounded; buildings and whole streets grew up like mushrooms, almost in a night. Every man carried a buckskin bag of gold-dust, and it was received as currency at a dollar a pinch. Everyone went armed. A stormy life ebbed and flowed through the town.[2]

chapter 3

The Comstock Lode

The Mother Lode was the name given to the gold deposits in California. The lode ran along the western side of the Sierra Nevadas. It was quickly overrun with miners. On the other side of the Sierra—the eastern side—there were but a few specks of gold on the surface and fewer prospectors. The terrain east of the mountain range was mostly dry and barren. This was the high desert country of the Utah Territory (later Nevada).

Throughout the 1850s, miners would pause for a few days on the eastern side of the Sierra to search for gold before continuing west to California's Mother Lode. Finding the yellow flakes scarce, they would move along. These miners had no idea that they were standing on a precious metal of another sort—silver!

They didn't know what silver ore looked like, so they simply shoveled it aside.

The few prospectors who did live in the high desert managed to scratch out a living. Among them was Henry Comstock, a gruff man who was nicknamed Old Pancake after his favorite food. One of Comstock's friends was James Finney, who was called Old Virginny. While staggering along the road drunk one night, Old Virginny dropped a bottle of whisky. When it smashed on the ground, he looked up and shouted, "I christen this ground Virginia!"[1] The town became known as Virginia City.

Comstock and Finney each had a claim of the legal size, measuring fifty feet wide and four hundred feet long. When the two miners found traces of gold in 1859, they named the area Gold Hill. They each made about twenty dollars a day—good money at that time.

Two Irishmen, Patrick McLaughlin and Peter O'Riley, showed up one day at Gold Hill. Finding the area claimed, McLaughlin and O'Riley hiked a short distance to Six-Mile Canyon, where they began to dig. About four feet down, they struck a layer of blue-black sand. Thinking nothing of it, they dug deeper until they found a pale dust. It was gold, they were sure, but

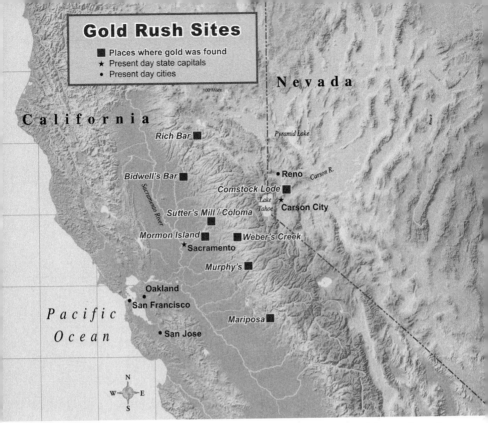

The Comstock Lode was one of many sites where gold was found during the gold rush. This map shows several gold rush sites.

something was wrong with it. The blue-black sand had lightened its color.

Henry Comstock showed up one day at Six-Mile Canyon. He inspected the pale flakes of gold and then claimed the area as his own. He said the Irishmen were on his ranch, which was a lie. Comstock would not allow them to continue digging unless he and a friend, Emanuel Penrod, were given half the profits. McLaughlin and O'Riley reluctantly agreed.

For the next month, the four miners tossed aside the blue-black sand to get to the pale flakes of gold. Each day they turned up hundreds of dollars in gold.

Finally, one month later, a settler on the Truckee River decided to have the blue-black sand examined. He carried a sack of it west over the Sierra to Grass Valley, California. The settler took the sand to an assayer, a person who examined the minerals to find out how much they were worth. The assayer could not believe the test results. The blue-black sand was worth $3,000 in silver and $876 in gold per ton.

By the next morning, it seemed that every citizen in Grass Valley had heard about the silver and gold. Hundreds of men raced across the Sierra to the high desert. There, they found the area from Gold Hill to Six-Mile Canyon already claimed.

When Comstock and his partners were told what they had, they celebrated. Comstock roamed up and down the area, bragging so loudly that the entire region of blue-black sand became known as the Comstock Lode.

James Finney was the first to sell his claim to the new arrivals from Grass Valley. Some say all he got in return was a horse, two blankets, and a bottle of whisky. Comstock soon followed, selling his claim for $11,000. He later invested the money in a supply store and lost it. A decade later, the poor man wandered to Montana, where he shot himself. Comstock's friend Penrod sold his claim for $8,500, then disappeared. McLauglin sold his share for $3,500. He became a cook for other miners and died penniless.

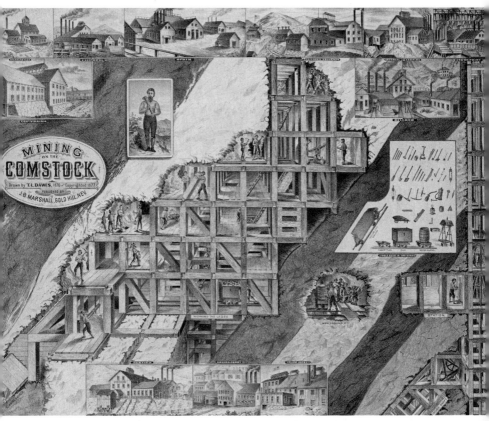

This 1876 drawing of the Comstock hillside shows the mine shaft, tunnels and supports, mining tools, miners doing various activities, and exterior views of several mining companies working the Comstock Lode.

O'Riley was smarter. He held on to his claim until he was offered $45,000, a sum he couldn't refuse. Soon, however, he went insane and began wandering the countryside, carrying a pick and shovel but never digging.

The newcomers kept their wits about them. They invested in heavy machinery and dug deep shafts. Thousands of miners from the Mother Lode joined them in the digging. More than $1 million worth of silver and gold was pulled up the first year, and twice that the second. The sum reached $6.24 million in 1862 and doubled again the next year. In 1869, a railroad was built from Virginia City to Nevada's territorial capital, Carson City, to haul supplies and the loot. A massive amount of metal worth $38.57 million was dug up in 1873—and it was immediately dubbed the Big Bonanza.

In the first thirty years, from the time the discoverers sold their claims until 1890, the Comstock Lode yielded nearly $400 million in silver and gold. Just as California is called the Golden State, the state of Nevada officially became the Silver State.

chapter 4

Other Western Rushes

On January 6, 1859, a few months before the rush for silver in Nevada, another discovery was made. As usual, it was more a matter of luck than anything else. A prospector named George Jackson had been roaming with his two dogs through the snowy Rockies in search of gold. Jackson was about thirty miles west of Denver, in what was then Kansas Territory (the Colorado Territory had not been established yet). The young prospector was an experienced miner, having spent several years working California's Mother Lode with the Forty-Niners. When Jackson ran out of food, he decided to quit exploring for gold. On his way back to Denver, he came upon a meadow where the snow had been melted by a hot spring. He decided to search for gold one more day.

Jackson tramped through the snow along the frozen south fork of Clear Creek. Then he saw it: a gravel bar that sparkled underneath the ice. He built a bonfire on the ice to thaw it. Then he reached in and broke off a chunk of the bar. When he swirled the dirt and rock in his drinking cup, a few tiny gold nuggets were left at the bottom.

He had no mining tools with him. The frozen ground was too hard to dig through anyway. Jackson covered up the signs of his discovery, then marked the place so that he could it find later. He would return to the area after the spring thaw by following his secret treasure map. When he reached Denver, then only a town of some twenty cabins, he wrote in his diary:

> After a good supper of meat—I went to bed and dreamed of riches galore in that bar. If I only had a pick and pan instead of a hunting knife and the cup. I could dig out a sack full of the yellow stuff. My mind ran upon it all night long. I dreamed all sorts of things—about a fine house and good clothes, a carriage and horses, travel, what I would take to the folks down in old Missouri and everything you can think of—I had struck it rich! There were millions in it![1]

Jackson was partly right. More than $100 million in gold would be lifted from the south fork of Clear

Creek, but he did not gain the riches he had imagined. In May, he returned with some friends to the area. In six days, they panned out $1,900 worth of gold. Soon after, Jackson sold his portion of the claim for a very small sum.

Jackson's discovery wasn't the first in the Rocky Mountain area. Tiny flakes of gold had been seen in these parts for a few years. The joint discoveries of the Comstock Lode and Clear Creek seemed to signal the start of a mad dash by more than one hundred thousand prospectors to the Colorado area. Hordes of experienced miners traveled from California, and thousands of novices poured in from the East. The rallying cry was "Pike's Peak or Bust"—named after the landmark mountain nearby.

Horace Greeley

Many Easterners were inspired by the newspaper stories of popular *New York Tribune* journalist Horace Greeley, who wrote firsthand accounts of the gold. Little did anyone know that Greeley had been tricked.

Greeley arrived in Denver determined to see the gold for himself. The townsfolk welcomed him and sent him off to a mining camp. Greeley was such a proud man that the miners decided to fool him.

One way to sell a worthless claim was to sprinkle flakes of gold dust in an area where a buyer was likely to pan. When he found the flakes, he was sure that the claim had gold in it. This was called "salting a claim."

When Greeley arrived at the camp, the miners already had salted an area for him. They showed him how to pan for gold properly. Greeley then proceeded to pan at the salted spot. At the bottom of his pan, he found several gold flakes. He panned a second time with the same sparkling results. "Gentlemen," he announced, "I have examined your property with my own eyes and worked some of it with my own hands and I have no hesitation in saying that your discovery is what it is represented to be—the richest and greatest in America."[2]

When he returned to New York, Greeley wrote about his trip in the same excited way. Then he gave this famous order: "Go west, young man." Plenty of people followed his advice.

Cripple Creek

Bob Womack was working on a ranch at Cripple Creek, Colorado, in 1878, when he found a small chunk of rock that contained gold. It appeared to have drifted down the creek. Womack had the chunk

Horace Greeley, a popular New York journalist, traveled to Denver, Colorado, to report on the gold rush. Although he reported that he had seen a lot of gold, he did not know that the miners had tricked him by salting the claim he visited.

assayed and found the gold to be worth $200 a ton. Now it was just a matter of finding the vein from which the chunk had come.

Womack spent the next decade wandering drunk around the area, digging holes for miles around. People laughed at him, and they called him Crazy Bob. His search paid off in 1890, when he struck the vein in Poverty Gulch, not far from where he had found the original chunk of rock. Cripple Creek had been explored by real miners years earlier, but no gold was found. The townspeople weren't about to believe Crazy Bob.

Womack didn't care. He started digging a shaft for his mine and eagerly showed the locals more chunks filled with gold. They refused to give him the money he needed to develop his mine. Instead, two other prospectors made strikes of their own totaling more than $200,000 worth of precious metal. The rush was on. By 1893, more than 10,000 prospectors were digging in the area. By 1900, Cripple Creek's population had swelled to 25,000, and $18 million in gold was found. Womack's mine produced more than $3 million, but Womack didn't get any of it. In a drunken state, Crazy Bob sold his mine for $300 and left the area. He died broke.

The Dakotas

In the late 1870s, two brothers, Moses and Fred Manuel, found rich deposits of gold near Deadwood in the Black Hills of the Dakota Territory. The Manuels mined what they could with their simple equipment. Then they sold their claim, which they had called the Homestake. The Manuels were paid $70,000 (a great sum at the time) for their mine and were instantly wealthy. Others certainly got rich off the mine as well. The Homestake Mine was probably the richest single mine in the world, eventually producing more than $1 billion in gold.

A view of the Homestake mining town. The Homestake Mine in the Black Hills of the Dakota Territory produced more than $1 billion in gold.

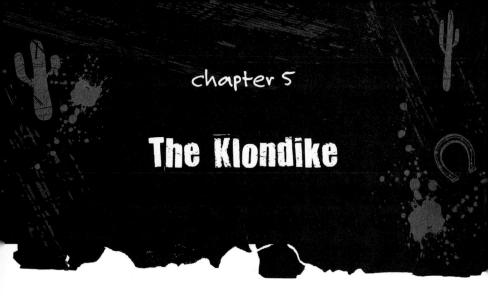

chapter 5

The Klondike

Gold fever reached its peak in 1897. Several dozen men sailed into Seattle, Washington, and came ashore with mounds of gold. This sight triggered the wildest rush for gold in the history of America. The headlines in the *Seattle Post-Intelligencer* read: "GOLD! GOLD! GOLD! GOLD!—Sixty Eight Rich Men on The Steamer *Portland*—STACKS OF YELLOW METAL!"[1]

One man tried to lift a suitcase so heavy with gold that the handle snapped off. Another gave his unsuspecting wife a sack that held $100,000 worth of gold—an enormous fortune. Another man and his son returned with $112,000 in gold.

Within weeks, everyone had heard of the Klondike. The Klondike is a part of the Yukon Territory in north-west Canada. It seemed as though every prospector in

America was on his way there. In 1897, at least two hundred thousand people set out for the Klondike. Most never made it. Getting there was a terrific ordeal.

Discovery

No more than a dozen prospectors panned for gold along creek beds in the Yukon Territory in 1870. Twenty years later, there were about 2,500 men looking for gold. In 1895, they managed to find more than $1 million in gold. Still, it wasn't enough to lure the grizzled veteran miners of California, Nevada, and Colorado. Too many of them had journeyed into hills before, only to come up empty-handed.

The frenzy began when an American named George Washington Carmack poured a shotgun shell of gold dust onto a saloon counter for all to see. Carmack and two American Indian friends, Tagish Charlie and Skookum Jim, had found a huge deposit of gold along Rabbit Creek.

Prospectors from Forty Mile and the nearby town of Dawson soon were panning along Rabbit Creek, which immediately was renamed Bonanza Creek. At Bonanza Creek, and a few miles south at Eldorado Creek, more than two tons of gold were found in the next few months. Carmack and his two friends would be among those who showed up in the Seattle harbor with hundreds of thousands of dollars in gold.

Getting There

The Klondike gold rush will forever be remembered not for the riches, but for the trip. All the work was in getting there.

There were two main ways to reach the town of Dawson from the south. One was to sail by steamer around the Aleutian Islands to Alaska's west coast, then 1,355 miles up the Yukon River. This could be difficult, because the Yukon is frozen much of the year. Once a boat reaches an icy portion of the river, it is locked in until the next spring's thaw. The other way to reach the town was to cross some of the most treacherous land on the continent. From the Skagway or Dyea ports in Alaska, miners crossed the Alaskan coastal range. They had to choose between White Pass, with its steep cliffs and ghastly swamps, or Chilkoot Pass, with its harrowing climb.

Prospectors hauled a ton of food and supplies with them. If they didn't, they would run out before the end of the six-month trip to Dawson. The last four miles over the Chilkoot were so steep that climbing them took almost all day. The job of hauling a ton of

A large group of prospectors bound for the Klondike are on the mountain path of Chilkoot Pass. The steep cliffs at the end of the pass claimed the lives of thousands of animals.

baggage over the pass, carrying no more than eighty pounds a day, sometimes took three months to finish. The route got so treacherous at times that men climbed on their hands and knees. Often, horses were used to climb White Pass, but there were so many hazards that thousands of the animals died along the trail.

Once over either the Chilkoot Pass or the White Pass, the miners had to cross a string of lakes and rivers. This was a frustrating task as well. One man hauled a ton of food and supplies over the Chilkoot to Lake Lindeman, where he built a boat. Rushing down the rapids, the boat crashed into a rock, and everything was lost. The man trudged back to the starting point, bought a new load of equipment, and spent another three months hauling it over the Chilkoot. He built another boat and again lost everything in the rapids. The man swam ashore, grabbed a gun, and killed himself.

Living in the North

Not everyone suffered such tragedy. By mid-1898, there were 28,000 people in Dawson. A few were women and children, but most were men hoping to strike it rich. They were known as Sourdoughs, because every prospector kept a bowl of sourdough bread starter in his cabin.

When winter arrived, the cold was devastating. The temperature sometimes dropped to 75 degrees below zero, while 38 degrees below was considered mild. In summer, it might warm up to 100 degrees. Below the ground there was a permafrost that never thawed, even in summer. It made digging in the Klondike all the more difficult. Each night, miners would build bonfires at the bottoms of their shafts, melting away perhaps six inches of ice by morning. Sometimes it took all summer to get deep enough to reach gold.

When a prospector hit pay dirt, he knew it. The ground was so rich with the precious metal that a single shovelful could yield $800. Some prospectors did indeed get rich. Fred Bruceth panned $61,000 in one day. Big Alex McDonald, who was known as "The King of the Klondike," once found a single gold nugget that weighed nearly four pounds. Lucky Swede Anderson was tricked into paying $800 for a supposedly worthless claim, but then got the last laugh when he dug out $1 million in gold from it.

As quickly as it started, however, the Klondike gold rush ended. There was little ground left to dig and far too many diggers. The gold was gone. Prospectors began leaving, first in a trickle, then in a rush. The Chilkoot and White Passes were nearly as clogged with people going as they had been with people coming.

Only one-fourth of the estimated two hundred thousand people who set out for Dawson made it there. Of those, only half looked for gold. Of the four thousand who found gold, maybe four hundred really got rich.

chapter 6

The End of the Rush for Gold

In the goldfields across the land, simple panning and wooden troughs eventually became obsolete. Big businesses with giant machinery moved in, replacing the crude methods of mining. With their chance of getting rich on their own now slim, prospectors began working for large companies that sifted through tons of dirt and rock each day.

Mining Becomes Big Business

Gold and silver deposits were known to be deep in the earth, but getting there required intensive labor. Enormous caves were dug using hand drills and sledges. Compressed-air drills were great for drilling holes into granite or quartz, but they stirred up clouds of razor-sharp particles that lodged in men's lungs and caused silicosis, an often fatal disease.

Miners journeyed deep underground to dig up ore from which gold and silver were removed. Stamping machines crushed the ore into a fine paste. The ore was then placed in large steam-heated pans, and the precious metals were chemically extracted.

Mining Dangers

Black gunpowder was often used to blast through rock. This powder was packed into a hole generally the depth of a finger and ignited by a fuse. In the 1870s, dynamite replaced black powder. Dynamite was about four times as powerful as gunpowder. However, it was also more dangerous. Explosions sometimes caused cave-ins or released deadly fumes. When dynamite was introduced to mining, many more miners died than before.

One story in an 1891 Colorado newspaper told of four men who were "torn and mangled beyond recognition" after an explosion in a Clear Creek mine.[1] Mining explosions were so common that most never even made the news.

One occurred in 1900 at the Winter Quarters Mine in Scofield, Utah. More than three hundred men were in the No. 1 and No. 4 shafts when a low thud was heard. Black powder had exploded, filling the shafts with a deadly gas. In moments, more than two hundred men were killed. Death came so quickly that some miners died while still holding their tools.

Why did prospectors risk their lives in such dangerous exploits? Most did it in the hope of someday striking it rich, not just because they wanted to live as rich men, but also for the thrill of finding wealth.

Settling the West

The mining boom did something else as well. It led to the settlement of the West. Before the gold rush in 1849, the California non-American Indian population was about fourteen thousand. A dozen years later, it had ballooned to 380,000. Gold was discovered in Columbia, California, in March 1850. A month later, the town had grown from 300 to 8,000 people. By the end of that same year, Columbia had 30 saloons, 143 gambling houses, 53 stores, 4 hotels, and 4 banks. Virginia City, where Old Virginny had dropped a bottle of whisky and named the town, exploded in the early 1860s into a metropolis of 20,000 people, which included 3 undertakers, 4 churches, 100 saloons, and about 19,000 starry-eyed miners.

For every prospector who struck it rich, there were a hundred or more who died poor. Most of the time, mining was a thankless, luckless, punishing business. Each miner, no matter what his fate was, had a story to tell, the same story of being close to fabulous wealth, having the riches within reach, and trying to improve his lot in life. It was the story of miners.

In 1954, prospector James Williams stumbled across a lost mine in the hills around Salmon City, Idaho. The mining tunnel he found was so old that in the middle of its entrance was a tree that had lived more than fifty years. Inside, Williams found its walls so rich in gold that he could pick out nuggets with his fingertips. Why was the gold still there? What had happened to the owner of the mine? He may have been killed by a bear, a bandit, or another miner. Or he simply may have lost his way back to the mine.

The gold rush changed the landscape of the West dramatically. Barren land and sleepy rural areas became bustling boomtowns. This illustration shows the main street of Virginia City, Nevada, in the 1870s at the height of the mining of the Comstock Lode.

Chapter Notes

Chapter 1. A Golden Discovery

1. Ralph K. Andrist, *The California Gold Rush* (London: Prentice-Hall International, 1961), p. 18.
2. Ibid.
3. Ibid., p. 19.
4. Gordon V. Axon, *The California Gold Rush* (New York: Mason/Charter, 1976), p. 13.
5. Ibid., p. 29.

Chapter 2. The California Gold Rush

1. Vardis Fisher, *Gold Rushes and Mining Camps of the Early American West* (Caldwell, Idaho: Caxton Printers, Ltd., 1968), p. 98.
2. Ibid.

Chapter 3. The Comstock Lode

1. Robert Wallace, *The Miners* (New York: Time-Life Books, 1976), p. 60.

Chapter 4. Other Western Rushes

1. Robert Wallace, *The Miners* (New York: Time-Life Books, 1976), p. 19.
2. Vardis Fisher, *Gold Rushes and Mining Camps of the Early American West* (Caldwell, Idaho: Caxton Printers, 1968), p. 69.

Chapter 5. The Klondike

1. Robert Wallace, *The Miners* (New York: Time-Life Books, 1976), p. 206.

Chapter 6. The End of the Rush for Gold

1. Robert Wallace, *The Miners* (New York: Time-Life Books, 1976), p. 103.

Glossary

assayer—A person who tests mineral ores to see if they contain any valuable metals.

backer—A person who provides the money for mining a claim. A miner would do the actual panning and would share the gold with the backer.

claim—A piece of land that a miner has made his own. All the rights to the minerals in that claim are his. A typical claim was about fifty feet by four hundred feet.

cradle—A long wooden trough used by miners to separate gold flakes and nuggets from mud and silt from the bottom of a creek bed. They would fill the trough with mud and water, and then they would rock it until the mud separated from the heavier minerals, such as gold.

desperado—An outlaw.

fool's gold—A mineral that looks like gold but is worthless. Pure gold is soft and malleable and can be beaten into sheets. Fool's gold is hard and breaks apart if it is struck with a hammer. Its scientific name is pyrite.

grubstaking—Working a claim using money supplied by a backer. The miner does all the mining work, and the backer provides the money and tools needed to mine, getting a share of the gold that is found.

lode—A mineral deposit.

long tom—A mining device resembling many cradles attached to one another. Mud was thrown into the trough, and water was poured down. The mud would wash away, and the heavier gold would remain.

panning—Using a shallow, wide pan to search for gold. Scooping up water and mud from a creek bed, the miner would swish the water to separate the sand and dirt from larger rocks that might have been gold.

placer gold—Gold that is found at the surface of creek beds and can be panned easily.

salting—A practice used to sell a worthless claim. The seller sprinkled a few flecks of gold around the claim. When the buyer inspected the claim, he saw the planted flecks and may have thought the claim was valuable.

silt—The sediments deposited on the bottom of a creek or riverbed.

stake—Another name for a claim.

tailrace—A trough where minerals are separated from silt.

Further Reading

Books

Berton, Pierre. *Stampede for Gold: The Story of the Klondike Rush*. New York: Sterling Publishing Co., 2007.

Fradin, Dennis Brindell. *The California Gold Rush*. New York: Marshall Cavendish Children's Books, 2008.

Friedman, Mel. *The California Gold Rush*. New York: Children's Press, 2010.

Sonneborn, Liz. *The California Gold Rush: Transforming the American West*. New York: Chelsea House, 2009.

Thompson, Linda. *The California Gold Rush*. Vero Beach, Fla.: Rourke Publishing, 2005.

Internet Addresses

Eyewitness to History.com: The California Gold Rush, 1849
<http://www.eyewitnesstohistory.com/californiagoldrush.htm>

Oakland Museum of California: Gold Rush! California's Untold Stories
<http://museumca.org/goldrush/>

PBS: American Experience—The Gold Rush
<http://www.pbs.org/wgbh/amex/goldrush/>

Index